Dare to Dream

LUCIE MUCHINA

Dare to Dream
Copyright © 2019 Lucie Muchina

All rights reserved. No part of this publication may be reproduced, stored in a retrieval system, or transmitted, in any form or by any means, electronic, mechanical, photocopying, recording or otherwise without the prior permission of Lucie Muchina.

All Scripture quotations, unless otherwise indicated, are taken from the Holy Bible, New International Version, UK edition, copyright © 1973, 1978, 1984 by International Bible Society. Published by Hodder and Stoughton. Used by permission. All rights reserved.

Scripture quotations marked NLT are taken from the Holy Bible, New Living Translation, copyright © 1996, 2004, 2007 by Tyndale House Foundation. Used by permission of Tyndale House Publishers, Inc., Carol Stream, Illinois 60188. All rights reserved. www.newlivingtranslation.com | www.tyndale.com

Scripture quotations marked NKJV are taken from the New King James Version. Copyright © 1982 by Thomas Nelson, Inc. Used by permission. All rights reserved.

ISBN: 978-0-9928315-1-6

Contents

Introduction 5

Tabby: The Girl with a Big Heart 7

Life in Secondary school 11

Home Sweet Home 19

Life at College 21

The Drive to Change 23

Does God Exist? 29

I'm in Love 31

Conclusion 33

Introduction

Dreams have the ability to take us to a realm that confounds our minds. The good news is that everyone has the ability to dream and create a world personal to them. This book introduces a young woman named Tabby who dared to dream and subsequently turned her life around.

Tabby is a shortened version of Tabitha, a Hebrew name which means Beauty or Grace. Beauty is a combination of qualities that pleases the aesthetic senses. Grace on the other hand refers to unmerited favour, a kindness from God that we do not deserve. Tabby's beauty is clearly demonstrated from her outward appearance as well as her inner self. Her community sing praises for the wonderful girl she is.

The story of Tabby albeit from a different cultural background resonates with the lives of most people. From growing up in a disadvantaged home to challenges in her academic life and finally to a failed marriage,

Tabby's life appears to be pushed from pillar to post with little or no way out. She is faced with a choice of giving up altogether and returning to live with her parents, or pushing through the difficult circumstances she faces. She lives up to her name and perseveres all the way. She refuses to give up setting a clear example that with God's help and self-determination, one can achieve their hearts desires.

The aim of the story is to encourage the reader and especially those who may be going through challenges in their journey of life. Tabby is depicted as one who sees a silver lining in every cloud and reminds us that even in desperate circumstances where dreams are lost, one can dream again. The clear message is "never to give up" as there's always light at the end of the tunnel.

In Christ's Love,

Lucie Muchina

Tabby:
THE GIRL WITH A BIG HEART

Born and bred in a humble background, Tabby grew up on a farm in a remote part of an African village. A second-born child in a family of seven and the eldest of the girls, she took on the responsibility of an older sibling from an early age. Her father worked as a technician in a local hospital and her mother, who was a qualified teacher, opted to stay at home to bring up all seven children whose demands were high given the proximity in their ages.

Tabby grew up to be an exemplary young woman. She was 5 ft 6 inches tall, short dark hair and with the most dazzling eyes. She had a particular love for music and could be heard singing in the calm of the night. Despite growing up in a large family, Tabby was a timid girl. She was known for her humility and hard work. As the eldest sister, she took on most of the household duties and helped her mother in any and every task that was required of her. This included waking up early to help with milking cows, then selling the milk to local shops before going to school. She did this daily. After school, Tabby would rush home to help her mother with preparation of evening meals, among other chores. Such was her diligence that she earned her nickname 'Mzuri' by locals, a term which meant 'good'. No child in the neighbourhood could match up to Tabby's good behaviour.

Despite a busy schedule at home, Tabby attended school like every other child of her age. Going to school was a great relief as it provided a respite from everyday household chores. Unfortunately, the demands at home led to Tabby occasionally arriving late to school. The punishment for lateness to school was caning and teachers would take no excuse for this "misconduct". In addition, caning was the frequently used method of punishment for children in Tabby's days. This could equally be meted out by neighbours or any adult who thought they fitted the description of the role of a 'parent'. Tabby feared being caned and would do whatever it took to avoid it. She was also well aware that any adult had every right to discipline any child in the neighbourhood. In one unforgettable incident, a neighbour had caned her for not completing a task on time. This happened when Tabby and her siblings had been left in the neighbour's care whilst her parents were away. The caning, which resulted with facial injuries had left Tabby very distraught. Why would anyone want to punish Tabby of all children? It was therefore no surprise she could not wait to finish primary education and start high school. As far as she was concerned, there was more freedom and fewer canings if any, from teachers and others in secondary education!

The cycle of getting to school late and leaving in a rush to get home and help her mother was Tabby's lifestyle in primary education. Tabby would walk long distances to fetch water with containers tied to her back and return home late. She would be so tired that reading would be the last thing on her mind, never mind the lack of time to even do so. The chores and the lateness to school left Tabby desperate to leave home and in search of a childhood life she had so missed. Now she was in her last year in primary education, she didn't have long to wait. In six months', time, she would get her results which would give her a chance to get into secondary school.

Life in Secondary School

Tabby obtained good-enough grades from primary school and was admitted to a part privately funded school. What a relief after many years of hard work in her rural home! She visited the big city and made new friends. She was equally looking forward to a new way of life and some freedom...at last!

However, her first day at school was nerve racking as Tabby didn't have a clue what to expect. It didn't take long for her to realise that most of her classmates wore a similar style of shoes, something she attributed to the fact they lived around the city and were more acquainted to urban trends. Wearing shoes was now mandatory, not optional - a life she had been used to in primary school. She soon realised that there was an expected etiquette in the new world. Her hair had to be well groomed and so was her facial make up. This was a silent expectation from her peers. Life was changing too fast for Tabby. She needed to commute by bus to her new school and had to learn the route to school sooner rather than later.

Due to her home being miles away from her new school, Tabby's parents had her live with her grandma who lived closer to her school. This seemed a good idea and Tabby agreed to visit her home every weekend. With everything in place, Tabby packed up her few belongings and said goodbye to her siblings and looked forward to a new life at grandma's home.

LIFE AT GRANDMA'S

Tabby moved in with Grandma with mixed emotions. Part of her wanted to remain at home with her siblings and the friends she had grown up with. The other part of her was keen to go to Grandma's as a solution to the tortuous journey to school from her home which was exacerbated by lack of public transport and a long walking distance. Grandma's house was well presented and on the high street. The home had good access to public transport. There was little walking required on Tabby's part. Tabby was given her own room, something she was not used to (she was used to sharing one room with two other siblings). Being alone in a room would be the first hurdle and she had to adjust quickly. The saving grace was that she would look forward to weekends when she would spend time with her family.

The new environment at Grandma's was one of the few challenges Tabby had to overcome among other challenges including adjusting to city life which was a whole new experience. She was also entering puberty and becoming aware of her body changes. Local boys and in particular "Herbert" from her school were showing an interest and teasing her, which made her feel very uncomfortable. Her father had made it clear and in no uncertain terms that no "boyfriends" were allowed before completion of school and only he was to give the go-ahead to any relationship. Therefore, as far as Tabby was concerned, there was no chance of even looking at a boy! This was a 'no go' zone.

In the initial months after moving into Grandma's, Grandma was friendly and loving. She treated Tabby as her own and would give her sweet treats which made Tabby settle down quickly. Tabby's aunt and uncle lived in the home which provided some social networking after school. Tabby also got to know the children around Grandma's neighbourhood who were of similar age to her. Life was changing for the better at last - or so she thought.

However, as weeks turned into months, Grandma started getting cold towards Tabby. The sweet treats were no more and Grandma was gradually becoming someone Tabby was afraid of. Grandma started turning off water taps and locking Tabby up in her bedroom. Tabby could not have a morning wash and would end up going to school without breakfast or a bath. She would have to wash her face in the school's toilet sinks and tidy herself there. Food became scarce and Tabby had to rely on the lunch money her father would provide on a monthly basis to cater for other meals in the day. Grandma was indifferent, she would not talk to Tabby or even look at her sometimes. This made Tabby feel so lonely and scared. What had gone so wrong and so quickly? she would ask herself. Such was Grandma's behaviour that at one point and over a period of several weeks, Grandma would give Tabby food which had been left out for a long time and had gone off.

Tabby was distraught, and with no one to talk to, resolved to keep these issues within herself until the weekend when she would go to her parents. She would break into tears on reaching home and tell her parents what had happened to her. In the initial stages, Tabby's parents thought this was a teething problem which would settle with time. However, as this continued, Tabby's parents moved Tabby from Grandma's to maintain good family relationship whilst preserving Tabby's emotional stability. The only option for Tabby was to live with her uncle during the second term of her secondary school. Tabby's uncle lived next door to her Grandma and therefore not much fuss was required to move over. It later turned out that Grandma was having early symptoms of dementia which explained her unusual behaviour.

LIFE AT UNCLE'S

Ted Wait was well known by the family as an easy-going man, full of humour and had much love for the drink. The nickname 'Wait' was commensurate to his character-he would not let anyone speak whilst he talked! His favourite word was 'wait' and anyone who conversed with him had to 'wait' or be interrupted before they said a word. Ted enjoyed visits to the local pub where most of his friends hanged around. They would spend endless hours drinking and would be heard laughing from the distance. His laughter amidst enjoyment of liquor was such that his elderly aunts (who lived nearby) at one time thought their home was being burgled and dogs were barking fiercely - only to realise that this was their one and only Ted laughing at the local bar!

Tabby was familiar with Ted's character and had previously seen Ted verbally and physically fight with her younger brother over ten pence! She therefore guessed what to expect. She was welcomed to Ted's home by Ted's wife and introduced to the house help, Monica. She was to share a room with Monica and spend most of her time with her. Monica was friendly to Tabby and felt sorry for what Tabby had had to endure at a young age. It didn't take long before Tabby noted that Ted's drinking was impacting on the family and money was in short supply. There were frequent altercations between Ted and his wife because of lack of food. Ted would also borrow money from Tabby. This was her transport and lunch money which her father would have provided upfront. Ted knew well enough and better not to borrow money from his niece not least because he was equally getting Tabby's payment for lodging.

In the weeks that followed, Ted borrowed money from his niece and promised to pay back. This was never the case and Ted would fail to honour his promise until a day before Tabby's cash run out. He would also pay the money back in the smallest denominations available which would end up confusing young Tabby and made it difficult for her to work out whether all what had been borrowed was paid back. This went on until the end of Tabby's second term in her first year of school. By this time and due to domestic issues in the home, Ted's wife left the home and Tabby was left to decide whether to continue living with her uncle or move house again.

Tabby was by now getting fed up with life at her extended family's home. She was getting home sick, and the pressure was taking a toll on her. She had only made it into the first two terms in secondary school and it felt like she had been there for years. Her parents had to decide yet again where she would stay for her third term. They agreed that her mum's aunts who lived near Uncle Ted would be the last option. Should this fail, Tabby would have to go back to her home in the farm and have to trek the two-mile journey before catching a bus to school. Things were not getting any easier for Tabby.

AT BIG GRANDMA'S

The two elderly sisters lived next door to each other. They were both advanced in age and close to each other. Aunts Mabel and Molly were their names. Mabel had an only daughter, Hagor, who had two children. One of these children was the same age as Tabby. Hagor was a single mother and provided support for both aunts. Both aunts loved Tabby and did their best to keep her happy. They had by this time learnt the problems young Tabby was facing in her brief encounter with her extended family and were therefore determined to make things easier for her.

Unfortunately for Tabby, Hagor had a different plan. She saw Tabby as a good source of labour. Tabby was expected to fetch water for the family from a nearby well, a good one and a half miles from her new home. She was expected to do the washing up, something that her new-found cousins were not allowed to do. She thought she had ran away from the chores in her primary education only to discover she was now a part-time house help for the new home. She was also not entitled to any delicacies; these were reserved for her cousins. She soon realised how different she was being treated and this upset her. In one of her journeys to school, Tabby forgot to carry her bus ticket. She had to go back to the new home, only to find her cousins sitting at the dining table and having a decent breakfast which had been unavailable to her only a few minutes beforehand. This broke her heart. She couldn't believe what was happening to her.

The realisation of this unequal, unfair treatment was too difficult for young Tabby to comprehend and as she walked back to the bus stop, she contemplated taking her own life! She thought it was easier to do away with life rather than have to go through what she was going through. She determined not to share this with anyone except her parents who were by now accustomed to her weekend tears of pain. Her parents had by this time decided that Tabby would come back home, no matter the difficulties in travelling to school. Soon the third term came to a close and Tabby made her way back home, a wounded girl having gone through the first year of secondary school with many disappointments. The years ahead were uncertain but Tabby had to take a day at a time.

Home Sweet Home

Going back home was a great sigh of relief. Tabby so needed to feel loved and cared for. She was only thirteen and had already been through so much. She knew commuting to school from home would not be an easy journey. Public transport was rare in those days and in most occasions would not accept children on board. Tabby had to accompany her uncle (who worked at another school near her secondary school) to be allowed on public vehicles. She remembered the evening chores and hoped these would not resurface even though they were nothing compared to what she had experienced.

Tabby was now in her second year in secondary school when she made her first journey from home-the place she called home! All went well even though the journey was no match to her grandma's home. There were challenges with getting onto buses which were often unpredictable and – when they arrived, would be full. As days went by, she got used to the long journeys and would plan her journey upfront. Commuting from home was most difficult when it rained. The roads would become impassable and Tabby would end up in school with mud all over her shoes. This was a huge embarrassment given her age and when looks mattered more than anything else. In one of those days after it had rained heavily, Tabby was walking the same route as she would normally take. She reached a rocky part of the road and heard what sounded like a motorbike's engine running. On looking back, she saw a huge fire which seemed to stem from an electric post. The scene scared her to death. She made every attempt to run but her muddy shoes wouldn't let her. There was no one else on the road which made her more terrified. She thought she was about to die; she tried to run and did not turn back until she arrived at the bus stop. Was this real or was she dreaming? Had she had a Moses encounter of a 'burning bush'? She gathered herself up and walk as fast as she could to the bus stop. There she met a few people waiting for the bus and asked them whether they had seen the same fire. To her surprise, no one had seen the fire. Was this real or something spooky? This added to her fear of walking to the bus stop on her own. She was to later learn that this was electric fire caused by heavy rains with electric wires running overhead.

Years went by amidst difficulties in commuting to school. Tabby knew that, whatever the challenges, she had to persevere and get through secondary school. Soon Tabby was sitting her final exams. She did brilliantly and was offered a place at a local college to study a diploma in hotel management. She had waited for this far too long.

Life at College

Life at college was fast. Tabby met students from other parts of the country who took similar or different courses from her. Most of the students seemed "au fait" with city life. Keen to get through her education and start earning, Tabby settled in very quickly. The thought of being in employment would bring a ray of hope to her life and help her forget those terrible memories.

College was an interesting world. This is where Tabby first understood what 'dating' meant after seeing different students dating. She knew though that she had to remain "pure" until such time when she got married. She was still a-shy girl, but it didn't take long for one of the boys to take an interest in her. This was like a terrible dream as she remembered her father's words of wisdom; "Never talk to boys unless they will marry you". How would she know unless she spoke to them?..she would ask herself.

Her first date didn't last long because the boy was abusing alcohol, something Tabby detested strongly thanks to her Christian upbringing. Soon after, Tabby joined the college choir and there she met Joe, a fellow student who had taken an interest in her and also loved music. Joe was a handsome 6 ft tall man. He sang male Tenor and this melted Tabby's heart. They both got on so well and would be seen strolling around the college. Tabby finally completed her course and took up a job locally. After working for a few months, she soon realised that overseas offered better opportunities in the hotel industry. Believing in herself, she applied to go to Mauritius and work as a receptionist in a hotel. To her excitement, the letter to confirm employment came through in no time.

The Drive to Change

Things were looking good and Tabby was happy with doors opening before her. Planning to move to a foreign country brought mixed feelings of excitement. On one hand, Tabby was keen to leave the old world which according to her, was nothing much to fall back to, other than painful memories. On the other hand, there was this new world opening up for her in a foreign land. She could work hard and support her parents. To add to the excitement, Tabby was by now engaged to Joe whom she planned to marry. The choice to fly out of the country at such a time was difficult but Tabby finally agreed with Joe, her fiancé, that this was the best thing to do. They were to get married and she would invite her husband to join her. The plan was then to start a family and live happily thereafter, or so she thought.

Beginning life in Mauritius was not as easy as Tabby thought. Home sickness took its toll and she would pack her bags several times 'ready to go back home', before settling down to the fact she had to face the challenges of her new life. Her new employers also took advantage of her and would pay her including all foreigners far less than the local people during the probation period. Had she made the right decision by moving to a foreign country? She also missed Joe so badly that she suffered from stomach ulcers and couldn't wait for her wedding.

She would spend hours talking to Joe on the phone and writing him love letters. Joe completed college and took up a job as a salesman. By this time, the couple had agreed to plan a wedding so that Joe could join Tabby in Mauritius. Joe's wages were based on the number of sales made and, on most occasions, he was not doing well financially. Despite this, the wedding had to go ahead, and they were both as determined as ever to get married. Tabby had to work extra hard to ensure this happened.

Days dragged into months but she determined that she would hold tight to her wedding day when all this loneliness would change. Soon her wedding day came. A dream come true. Tabby was all praises to her Almighty God. At last a lifetime companion and her dream of starting a family would be a reality.

Tabby travelled back to her homeland and, with the help of family and friends, married her sweetheart Joe. It was a day never to be forgotten. There was plenty to eat, not to mention the celebrations all through the night. The marriage was blessed by the church ministers and off they went on honeymoon. Three weeks later, Tabby had to say goodbye to her new husband and go back to Mauritius. She would then arrange for her husband to join her at a later date.

Joe's finally here

Fortunately, it didn't take long for Joe to be granted appropriate travel documents to join his wife Tabby. What a time of joy when the couple got together ready to start a new life together. By this time, Tabby was in a permanent job and earning a decent wage. Joe soon settled down and life couldn't be better. Tabby had finally found what she had all along yearned for. They toured the country visiting most of the exotic places. They made new friends and Joe got a job and was equally getting sufficient money. After two years, their first child was born – a girl – and, a year later, another little girl was born. With two children in the house, the couple closed the chapter of getting any more children. Bringing up children brought new challenges especially around childcare. They would alternate their working hours to accommodate child care, a task Joe struggled the most with. In his spare moments, Joe joined friends in a local pub and would spend endless hours drinking, only to come home late at night. He failed to go to work and also got into wrong company involved in drugs and crime. The humble, quiet man turned violent, abused alcohol and was never home. He had become verbally and physically aggressive towards Tabby and at one point picked up a metal object to hit her. Tabby was terrified, confused, depressed and lonely and in fear. She didn't know what to do. Should she leave this man, or return to her native land? Everything looked dark with no way out.

IT HURT SO BAD

Tabby decided to hang in there, hoping that Joe was going through an adjustment to new life and that he would soon change and be a responsible husband/father. She had to work out how to look after her little ones mostly on her own as Joe was never home most of the days. She was still aching from inside. The Tabby that was very excited with her new world had now become totally withdrawn. Her failing marriage was equally becoming the talk of the town. Those who knew her would talk in hushed voices and those who were brave enough would ask her directly what was happening to her marriage. There was no one to help her. She recalled a common phrase used by most of the women when she sought help: 'We all have tough times…this may have to be your cross to carry'. She fondly remembered her father and wondered what his response would be in this situation. This was the one man that loved her unconditionally–and saw the best in her. She also remembered the teaching in the church that God was her father. Would God give her the same response? She determined not to share her pain with anyone, not even with friends and family, as she didn't know who to trust. She almost lost her job as she had to stay at home looking after the children with no child care available. Things got from bad to worse. In one of those moments, Joe came in the night in a drunken state and, having no key to get into the house, smashed and broke the glass front door. Tabby came in from work in the morning to find a big hole in the door. Joe had by this time lost his job and Tabby had to get the door fixed, with or without money.

Tabby's faith kept her strong. She had by this time found a friend in the local church where she spent most of her time. She also regularly attended prayer meetings. This is where she would empty her woes in tears. She would then go home and cry herself to sleep. What had befallen this lovely young woman? Her dreams of youth were falling apart before her eyes. She thought she had gone through enough heart ache in her youth! She held on to prayer and prayed that Joe would change at some point. Meanwhile finances in the house went from scarce to none. This made things worse and she didn't have money even for gas and electricity! This was not the life Tabby was looking for. Do all married couples go through this, she wondered? Does God listen to tears or prayer? Joe had by this time come up with a myriad of 'reasons' why he couldn't work in a foreign country and was now travelling frequently back to their native land to look for work there. Had he given up on his marriage and family? Could things be this bad? What about Tabby and the children? Should they abandon the dream of working in a foreign country and go back to their native country?

Had they made the right choice? Was Tabby to go back to what she was running away from?

It soon became clear to Tabby that the reason Joe kept going back to their native land was that he had met another woman and had made her pregnant! Unbeknown to Tabby, Joe was living a double life! This was Tabby's worst nightmare. She recalled their wedding day, the vows they had made to love and cherish each other and how she had looked forward to family life. Amid all this, Tabby had to look after their two children and work to support the family, now being the sole bread winner. Tabby couldn't handle this and went down with depression. She would have lost her job if it hadn't been for her very 'understanding' manager. Her close friend from church kept her in her prayers and would pop by to see her and encourage her and help look after her two children when she needed to work.

Does God exist

Left in a quagmire, in a foreign land and crashed dreams, Tabby was lost for words in her new world. As far as she was concerned, there was either no God or, if He was there, He had forgotten about her. She would cry herself to sleep and only bring herself together when her children were around her. The same was the case when she went to church. She cried throughout the whole service, something other people saw as being 'overtaken by the Holy Spirit', but this was far from the truth. Such was Tabby's misery that few people wanted to hang around her. This was soon to come to an end when, thanks to the prayers of her friend, Tabby had an encounter with a man she recognised as Jesus. On this night, Tabby was sitting with a group of people from different nations. They had all converged to sing, something Tabby loved to do. In this dream, Tabby was sat on Jesus' lap and they were all singing heavenly songs. On waking up from this dream, Tabby's life was totally changed. She had had an encounter with the life changer! How she longed for this experience to last forever.

If anyone is in Christ, he is a new creation, the old has gone, the new has come (2 Cor 5:17 NIV). Tabby experienced a new lease of life. She had to start by doing what was an impossibility-forgiving her estranged husband. She had learnt that she needed to forgive so she could walk free and also be forgiven herself (Mathew 6:12). This was Tabby's longest and toughest journey. How could she forgive a man who had betrayed her? A man who turned his back on her and deserted her in her greatest time of need. Was it ever possible to totally forgive? Her new prayer partner, Mel, prayed with her and taught her the power of spoken words. That life and death is in the tongue's power (Proverbs 18:21). Tabby started professing forgiveness not just for her estranged husband but her extended family who had mistreated her in her youth. Her healing was gradual, and she could pray for those who had hurt her. This was the beginning of her breakthrough. Tabby's life changed for the better. She was promoted at work, her singing career grew and she recorded music and toured the country. Soon Tabby was blossoming and scaling new heights in what was previously a non-existent lifestyle.

I'm in Love

Unbeknown to Tabby, one of the guys she toured the country with, was in love with her. Tabby thought this was another bad dream. She couldn't remember when she last heard anyone say those magical words 'I love you' and meant it. Things were moving too fast for her. Tim was a great singer and played the bass guitar. This was a perfect match that would see the two travel the world doing what they loved – play music. Tim knew of Tabby's previous experience and was in no hurry to wed her. He knew that he had to gain Tabby's trust before they could move forward.

As time went by, Tabby got engaged to Tim and they planned a wedding together. Her wedding was a spectacular occasion that was graced with musicians from across the country. Tabby was married again – but this time to a man who loved her and shared similar interests. Tim was great with the children and settled easily into the new home. Tabby was however keen to support women who had gone through similar experiences as herself. She knew there were women who were not so privileged and had also experienced difficult times in their marriage or relationships. This would be her new world, one where only she understood having lived the life. Tim assured her of his support to do whatever she wanted to do. Tabby had finally found a lover and a companion! Her new-found faith grew stronger. There is a God in heaven after all! She exclaimed. And He had been real to her. She was now on a mission - to tell others her story, and Tim was part of it.

Conclusion

Tabby's experience is not uncommon. The nature of life is such that no one is immune to disappointment, frustration or betrayal. The ability to handle difficult situations and remain strong is remarkable. Unfortunately, not everyone is able to do this. For some people, difficult circumstances provide a good recipe' for depression, isolation and in extreme cases, some take their own lives.

Life experiences are not designed to break us. With the right help they have the potential to make us better and stronger people. The bible reminds us in 1 Cor 10:13 that "No temptation has overtaken you except what is common to mankind. God is faithful. He will not let you be tempted beyond what you can bear. But when you are tempted, He will also provide a way out so that you can endure it". This promise assures us that God is always in control of our lives and has a plan even when we go through tough times.

We don't have to run from trouble, and when faced with challenging situations, we have the opportunity to rise above circumstances by how we handle the situation. Similar to Tabby, God sends people to help us at our point of need. Our part is to ask for God to help us identify these "angels" and cooperate with them.

Tabby found solace in the word of God. The bible tells us that the "Word of God is living and active, sharper than any two-edged sword..." Hebrews 4:12. Tabby learnt to speak the word of God into her life. The more she committed herself to seeking God, the smaller her problems became. With the help of friends from church she managed to get back to her normal self and her life was turned around.

It is my desire that your life will be turned around for the good as you recognise the potential you have to overcome every obstacle with God by your side.

www.ingramcontent.com/pod-product-compliance
Lightning Source LLC
Chambersburg PA
CBHW050450010526
44118CB00013B/1767